COOKING UP S'MORE CAMPFIRE FUN

Family Style

ISBN-13: 978-1-56383-544-5
Item #2915

**Printed in the USA
by G&R Publishing Co.**

Distributed By:

507 Industrial Street
Waverly, IA 50677

www.cqbookstore.com

gifts@cqbookstore.com

 CQ Products

 CQ Products

 @cqproducts

 @cqproducts

Campfire Cooking

Cooking on a Grate

The red tab indicates how you'll cook each recipe. Here are a few tips:

- Use heavy-duty foil or a double layer of regular foil for leak-proof campfire cooking (coat with cooking spray before use).

- Rotate foil packs often for even cooking.

- Soak wooden skewers in water before using.

- Cooking times depend on the heat of your fire, weather conditions, and how close your food is to the heat. Quicker isn't always better - watch food closely and move as needed for even heat.

- Precook pasta at home and toss with a little oil to prevent sticking; store in a cooler.

Simple Crafts & Fun Activities

Craft & Activity

The blue tab means you'll find an easy project to make and use at the campsite. Be sure to:

- Play games in an open area, safely away from the campfire.

- Supervise children closely when they're near the fire or using tools like scissors.

- Make projects as simple or sophisticated as you like - it's all about having fun!

Stuffed Potato Boats

You'll Need

Foil

Cooking grate

Pepper Jack or cheddar cheese slices

Precooked bacon strips

Butter, sliced

Garlic salt & pepper to taste

Ingredients

Large baking potatoes

Deli sliced turkey or ham

Toppings *(sour cream, sliced green onions & chives)*

1 Set each potato on a piece of oiled foil, large enough to wrap around it. Slice each 'tater crosswise into ¾"-thick slices without cutting all the way through. *(Save time at the campfire by partially baking your potatoes at home before slicing and stuffing.)*

2 Stuff meat, cheese, and bacon between the cuts and top with butter slices. Sprinkle with seasonings and wrap in foil. Cook on a grate over hot coals for 45 to 60 minutes, rotating several times, until tender and hot. Serve with lip-smacking toppings.

Rockin' Tic-Tac-Toe

Using fingernail polish, paint pens, or acrylic paints, paint five flattish rocks with one color or design and paint five more rocks in a different pattern; let dry. With a permanent marker, paint pen, or chalk, draw a tic-tac-toe grid on a stump or the cut side of a large log (or draw a grid in the dirt with a stick). Play a rousing game or two – the winner gets out of clean-up duty!

Hiking Games

Explore your camping area and play some games at the same time! Just create these simple game pieces before you leave home and you'll be ready for fun. *(Remember to discard any trash you find, tread lightly, and be sure to treat the great outdoors with respect.)*

Grab your bag, pill box, or Bingo game. Who can find the most stuff?

I Spy

Paint a rock with nail polish, permanent markers, and/or paint markers. One player hides the rock nearby and the other players try to find it. The hider can give a hint such as, "I spy with my little eye the rock, hidden up high." Let the finder hide it next.

Bingo

Draw *(or download and print)* some plain bingo cards. Add words or pictures of things you'd find or hear while camping *(include nature and human-made items and make each card different)*. Make photocopies and give each player a card and marker. Search for the items on your card and cross off each one you find.

Scavenger Hunt

Make a list of small things players could find around a campsite; tape it to a paper bag *(or attach labeled stickers to removeable pill box sections)*. Be as specific or general as you want, for example, "2 red rocks," "something smooth," or "something starting with R." Then take a hike to collect these tiny treasures.

serves 4

Campfire Shortcake

Stir together 2 C. biscuit baking mix, ¼ C. melted butter, and ¼ C. heavy cream until just mixed. To cook in a pie iron, roll dough into 3" balls, flatten slightly, and set each in a greased pie iron. Close iron and cook on hot coals until golden brown on both sides. Slice the shortcake and fill with sweetened strawberries and whipped cream. *(To cook on a stick instead, press walnut-size balls of dough around the end of a foil-covered stick until ¼" thick all over. Hold over hot embers until golden brown and done, turning often. Crumble into a bowl and add toppings.)*

serves 3-4

Haystacks

Dump a 1 (15 oz.) can of chili with beans into a saucepan and heat it on a grate over hot coals until bubbly. Pile corn chips on each serving plate and top with some of the chili. Add as much shredded cheddar or smoked cheddar cheese, shredded lettuce, diced tomato, sliced black olives, sour cream, and salsa as you like. So easy. So quick. So satisfying.

serves 8

Double Orange Rolls

You'll Need

Griddle or foil pan

Cooking grate

Ingredients

4 large oranges

1 (13.9 oz.) tube orange rolls with icing*

* You can also use the grand-size orange or cinnamon rolls, but you'll need extra-large oranges.

1 Cut the oranges in half and scoop out the insides with a spoon *(eat 'em or use them to make a fruit salad).*

2 Put a roll into each orange shell; set close together on the griddle and cover tightly with foil. Cook on a grate over medium coals for 20 to 25 minutes, rotating several times, until rolls are puffy and cooked through. Spread with icing and eat right out of the shell.

Bearly S'mores

Cut large and mini marshmallows in half; press one large 'mallow piece on a chocolate graham cracker square for the snout and add two mini marshmallow halves for the eyes. With a dab of chocolate frosting, fasten a chocolate chip ear on each upper corner and a nose on the snout; add mini chocolate chip pupils on the eyes. Smoosh a hot roasted marshmallow between the bear face and another cracker for chocolaty s'mores deliciousness.

Taco Pies

You'll Need

Pie Irons

Ingredients

12 (5") flour tortillas

Vegetable oil

⅓ C. refried beans

¾ lb. cooked taco-
seasoned ground beef

Diced onion

Shredded cheese *(we
used Enchilado & Cotija
Mexican cheeses)*

Your favorite taco
toppings

Fresh tomatoes, shredded cheese, jalapeños, and sour cream!

makes 6

1 Place a tortilla on one side of an oiled pie iron and smear it with a thin layer of beans. Add ¼ to ⅓ cup taco meat*, some onion, and plenty of cheese.

To save time at the campsite, precook the seasoned ground beef before you leave home.

2 Set a second tortilla over the filling and close the iron; trim off the excess tortilla with a knife. *(Feed the hungry birds and squirrels with your scraps, if you'd like.)*

3 Cook on medium coals, turning often, until tortilla is browned on both sides and filling is hot. Repeat with the remaining ingredients to make more tacos. Plop them onto plates and pile on the toppings.

Breakfast Bread Bowls

You'll Need

- Foil
- Cooking grate

Ingredients

- Lunch-size soft or crusty bread rolls
- Deli sliced ham
- Eggs
- Salt & pepper to taste
- Shredded mozzarella cheese
- Shredded cheddar cheese
- Chopped fresh parsley

1 Cut the top off each roll and scoop out the center to make a ½"-thick shell. This will become the bowl to hold all the breakfast goodness.

2 Line the inside of bowls with a layer of ham – cover the bread well so you won't have any leaks.

3 Crack an egg into each bread bowl *(poke the yolk if you'd like)*. Season with salt and pepper and sprinkle with both cheeses. Replace the tops.

4 Wrap snugly in foil and set packs on a grate over medium coals. Cook about 20 minutes or until eggs are done the way you like them, rotating often. Sprinkle with parsley before eating.

serves 5

Camping Éclairs

You'll Need

- Zippered plastic bag
- Foil-covered cooking stick
  (about 1" in diameter)

Ingredients

- 1 (3.4 oz.) pkg. instant vanilla pudding mix
- 1¾ C. milk
- 1 (7.5 oz.) tube refrigerated biscuits
- Spray whipped cream
- ½ can chocolate frosting

1 Whisk together pudding mix and milk until thickened. Pour into the plastic bag and keep cool. For each éclair, press two biscuits together and flatten well. Grease the foil end of stick with cooking spray and wrap dough evenly around it to make a tube about 4" long; pinch edges together.

2 Hold over medium coals and cook slowly until brown on all sides. Remove crust from stick. Cut off a corner of the pudding bag and pipe some pudding and whipped cream into each crust. Top with chocolate frosting.

Grilled Fruit

Peel, core, and slice a fresh pineapple to make 1"-thick rings. Brush both sides with vegetable oil and rub with apple pie spice, if you'd like. Grill on an oiled grate over hot coals until browned on one side. Flip and sprinkle with white and brown sugar; cook until glazed and tender. Serve with a dip made by stirring 2½ T. honey into a 6 oz. carton of plain yogurt. Grill unpeeled sweet-tart apples the same way – so good!

Bacon-Wrapped Chicken Strips

Push one end of a bacon strip onto a sturdy skewer. Thread a chicken strip onto the skewer accordion-style and wrap the bacon around it, attaching other end to tip of skewer. *(Secure with toothpicks if necessary.)* Repeat to make as many as you want. Grill the skewers on a well-oiled grate over hot coals, turning often, until bacon and chicken are done. Brush lightly with your favorite barbecue sauce and serve with more sauce for dipping.

* *Slice boneless, skinless chicken breasts into strips ½" to ¾" thick and 6" long, or buy chicken fingers or stir-fry strips that are already trimmed.*

serves 1

Hot Cheese Dip Singles

In a small zippered freezer bag, combine 2 oz. softened cream cheese, ¼ C. shredded Mexican cheese blend, 1 T. chopped green chiles, 2 T. sour cream, 1 T. chopped red bell pepper, and a dash of cayenne pepper; close the bag and mash everything together. Cut off one corner of the bag and squeeze all the cheesy goodness into a small foil pie pan. Cover with foil and seal well. Set the pan directly on warm embers for 15 minutes or until hot. Stir and serve with chips for dipping.

Bubble Snakes

You'll Need

Good-quality dish soap
  (we used Dawn)

Bowl

Water

Scissors

Empty plastic water
  bottle

Old sock

*Blow out slow & steady
for super-long snakes*

1 Squirt some dish soap into a bowl and stir in a little water *(or use the recipe below)*. With scissors, cut off the bottom of a bottle.

2 Stretch a sock over the cut end of bottle and fold the cuff back to hold sock in place *(or use a rubber band)*. Dip the sock end of bottle into soap mixture and then gently blow air through the lid end – but don't ever inhale!

Bubble Station

Mix 10 cups water, 1 cup good dish soap, and 1 cup light corn syrup in a large drink dispenser. Fill cups or bowls with bubble mixture and dip bubble wands into it to blow fantastic bubbles. *(Bend pipe cleaners into closed shapes, fasten straws together with a rubber band, or simply use canning rings.)*

serves 6

Jivin' Chivin' Corn

You'll Need

Foil
Cooking grate

1 C. shredded fresh or grated
  Parmesan cheese

Chili powder to taste

Salt & pepper to taste

Chopped fresh chives

Ingredients

6 ears sweet corn
½ C. mayonnaise

1 Husk and clean the sweet corn. Brush a thin layer of mayo over each ear and sprinkle generously with cheese. Season with a little chili powder, salt, and pepper.

2 Wrap each ear in foil and set on a grate over medium coals to cook for 20 to 25 minutes, turning occasionally, until kernels are tender and beginning to brown. Sprinkle with chives. Now this is summer eatin'!

Cinnamon Roll-Ups

Mix ¼ C. sugar and 1 T. cinnamon in a shallow bowl. Separate crescent roll dough into eight triangles. Starting at the short side, wrap each triangle around a cooking stick in a single layer, coiling dough and sealing ends well. Coat in cinnamon-sugar. Hold over the campfire, cooking slowly and turning often until golden brown and done. To add a glaze, mix ¼ C. powdered sugar with 2 or 3 T. water; drizzle over roll-ups.

Bacon Pancake Dippers

You'll Need

Funnel

Squeeze bottle *(we used an empty syrup bottle)*

Griddle or large skillet

Cooking grate

Ingredients

2 C. biscuit baking mix

3 T. sugar

2 tsp. baking powder

1 C. milk

2 T. vegetable oil, plus more for brushing

2 eggs

12 precooked bacon strips

Butter

Pancake syrup

makes 12

1 Before you leave home, combine the baking mix, sugar, and baking powder in an airtight container and pack it along on your trip. To cook, add the milk, 2 tablespoons oil, and eggs to the dry ingredients in container and whisk until well blended. Using a funnel, pour the batter into the bottle.

2 Heat the griddle on a grate over a medium-hot fire and brush generously with oil. Squirt batter onto the griddle in long oval shapes slightly shorter than a bacon strip; set one bacon strip on top of each. Squeeze more batter over the bacon.

3 Cook until golden brown on both sides, flipping once. Serve these dippers with butter and syrup.

Clouds? Creatures? What shapes are your cakes?

serves 6

Perfectly Peared

You'll Need

8 x 8" foil pan
Foil
Cooking grate

Ingredients

3 large ripe pears *(still firm)*
1 T. sugar

¼ tsp. cinnamon
½ C. granola
⅓ C. dried sweetened cranberries
¼ C. apple juice
Whipped cream or ice cream, optional

1 Halve the pears lengthwise and remove the cores, enlarging the dent in the center of each one. Arrange pears in the pan with cut sides up.

2 Mix the sugar and cinnamon in a small bowl and sprinkle evenly over pears. Fill the centers with granola and cranberries.

3 Drizzle juice over the filling in pears. Cover with foil and seal well.

4 Set the pan on a grate over hot coals to cook about 20 minutes or until warm and tender, rotating several times. Top with whipped cream and serve warm.

S'macos

You'll Need

Dutch oven lid

Ingredients

Vegetable oil

Flour tortillas, any size

Chocolate & butterscotch chips

Mini marshmallows

Shredded coconut or chopped pecans

Other favorite ingredients *(caramel bits, chopped candy bars, other baking chip flavors, chopped cherries, etc.)*

1 Set the Dutch oven lid upside down on hot coals and brush the surface with oil. Set tortillas on the lid until warmed, then flip over; top with chips, marshmallows, and coconut or nuts – plus any other ingredients you like.

2 Fold each tortilla in half and press it lightly. Cook until the insides are all warm and melty and the tortilla is lightly browned. Then make s'more s'macos!

Glow Bowling

Decorate a sturdy ball with glow-in-the dark tape or paint (we used a 6" soccer ball). Remove the labels from six empty plastic water bottles. When it's dark, follow package directions to activate one or two glow sticks for each bottle; drop them in and add water until bottles are about ⅔ full. Fasten the lids and set bottles in a triangle shape like bowling pins, 4" to 6" apart. Roll the ball to knock them over. Strike!

makes 4

Breakfast Biscuit Burgers

You'll Need

Large skillet

Cooking grate

Ingredients

1 C. biscuit baking mix

¼ C. shredded cheddar cheese

6 T. milk

1 T. vegetable oil, plus more for skillet

½ tsp. garlic pepper

4 to 8 brown-and-serve sausage patties

4 eggs

Salt & pepper to taste

Cheese slices

1 In a bowl, stir together baking mix, shredded cheese, milk, 1 tablespoon oil, and garlic pepper. Oil the skillet and set on a grate over hot coals.

2 Drop dough into the hot skillet to make four equal biscuits; flatten slightly. Cook 6 to 8 minutes, flipping once, until browned and no longer doughy. Remove and keep warm near fire.

3 Cook the sausage patties in the same skillet until hot and browned on both sides. Remove and keep warm.

4 Add more oil to the skillet and when hot, cook the eggs to desired doneness, seasoning with salt and pepper. Split biscuits in half and layer an egg, sausage, and cheese slice in between.

Marshmallow Games

Cup Launcher Cut off the bottom of a plastic or foam cup. Knot the end of a 9" or 12" balloon, then cut off its bottom. Stretch balloon opening over the bottom of cup and fasten with tape. Put a marshmallow in the cup, pull the knot back, and let go...3-2-1 TAKE-OFF!

Catapult Stack eight popsicle or jumbo craft sticks together and fasten with rubber bands on each end. Slide a jumbo crosswise between the two bottom sticks and set another one on top, ends even. Rubberband those two together, about 1" from the end. Set a 'mallow *(or pom pom)* on the extended end of the top jumbo, press down, and let go.

Tin Can Toss

Wash and upcycle some tin cans after mealtime. Just tie string snugly around the opening and add a string handle; decorate with colored tape and/or curly ribbon. Create a hanging rack from scavenged branches stuck into weighted cans or poked right into the ground *(you'll need two forked ones and a cross branch)* or stretch clothesline between two trees. Hang up the cans and let everyone take turns tossing whiffle or foam balls, pompoms, or sock balls into the cans. Want some friendly competition? Mark each can with a different point value and keep score.

serves 4-6

Pizza Skewers

You'll Need

Skewers

Foil

Cooking grate

Ingredients

⅓ C. vegetable oil

1½ to 2 T. Italian seasoning

8 to 14 oz. pizza dough *(we used 1 (13.8 oz.) tube refrigerated pizza dough)*

1 (12 oz.) pkg. fully cooked sweet Italian chicken sausage links

1 pt. grape tomatoes

6 to 8 oz. fresh mozzarella cheese, thinly sliced

Chopped fresh basil

Grated Parmesan cheese

Pizza sauce

1 Mix the oil and Italian seasoning in a large bowl. Unroll the pizza dough and press into a rectangle about 8 x 11". Cut into 1" squares.

2 Slice the sausage into ½"-thick pieces. Toss the dough, sausage, and tomatoes with the oil mixture until well coated.

3 On skewers, alternately thread several pieces of dough with sausage and tomatoes, leaving some space between them. *(Extra dough pieces? Just skewer them and grill separately as pizza bread bites.)*

4 Grill the skewers on a greased foil-covered grate over medium coals until dough is browned on all sides, covering with greased foil partway through cooking. Top with mozzarella; cover again and cook until melted. Sprinkle with basil and Parmesan and serve with sauce.

makes 8

Gator Dogs

You'll Need

Grill basket

Cooking grate

Ingredients

1 (8 oz.) tube crescent dough sheet

8 bun-length hot dogs

4 slices American cheese, halved

Ketchup & mustard

1 Unroll and flatten the dough sheet; cut into eight even squares *(big enough to wrap around hot dogs without covering ends)*. Top each square with a piece of cheese and a hot dog; wrap dough around dog, pinching edges to seal.

2 Line up the dogs in a greased grill basket. Close basket and set on a grate over warm coals *(or hold it by the handle)* to cook slowly until browned and bumpy on all sides. Open the basket and roll the dogs as needed for even cooking. Serve with ketchup and mustard.

Walking Stick

Find that perfect stick – tall enough to hold onto, sturdy enough to support you, and straight enough to help you hike. Wrap colorful washi tape, duct tape, or yarn around it in lots of fun designs and patterns; tie on some jingle bells if you'd like. Then go take a hike!

Campers' French Toast

You'll Need

Wide mouth quart-size mason jar

Foil

Parchment paper

Cooking grate

Ingredients

4 eggs

1 T. vanilla

1 tsp. cinnamon

1 C. milk

1 loaf English muffin toasting bread

1 C. fresh blueberries

¼ C. sliced almonds

Pancake syrup

Pure maple syrup – a perfect finish!

serves 6-8

1 Break the eggs into the mason jar. Add vanilla, cinnamon, and milk; seal the jar and shake until well blended.

2 Line a large sheet of foil with parchment paper and set the whole loaf of bread on top; fold up loosely around bottom of loaf so slices separate slightly. Arrange blueberries and almonds between slices and over the loaf. Shake the egg mixture again and slowly pour over the bread.

3 Seal foil around loaf, then wrap in another layer of foil. Set the pack on a grate over medium coals *(or directly in warm embers)* to cook slowly, about 40 minutes; rotate several times and flip once until evenly cooked and no longer soggy. Remove from heat and let stand 10 minutes. Serve with syrup.

serves 4

Lasagna Foil Packs

You'll Need

Foil

Ingredients

Butter

1 to 1½ C. pasta sauce

6 cooked & cooled lasagna noodles, halved

1 zucchini, sliced

Sliced fresh mushrooms

Diced onion

½ lb. cooked, crumbled ground beef *(or sausage)*

1½ C. shredded mozzarella cheese

Garlic salt & pepper to taste

Cooking spray

1 Place two pats of butter in the middle of a 12″ piece of greased foil and spread with a thin layer of sauce. Set a noodle piece on top and layer with some vegetables, meat, cheese, and seasonings.

2 Make a second layer of noodle, sauce, veggies, meat, cheese, and seasonings. Top with a third noodle and spritz it with cooking spray. Wrap the foil loosely around food and seal well.

3 Make three more lasagna packs, reserving a little sauce and cheese for Step 4. Set packs directly on warm coals to cook 10 to 15 minutes or until hot and tender, rotating often.

4 Remove packs from fire, open the top, and spread with reserved sauce and cheese. Close loosely and return to coals until cheese melts.

serves 4

Garlic-Cheese Potato Pokes

You'll Need

Large zippered plastic bag
Skewers
Foil

Ingredients

2 (15 oz.) cans whole potatoes

½ C. grated Parmesan cheese
¼ C. butter, softened
1½ tsp. garlic powder
½ tsp. Italian seasoning
Salt & pepper to taste
Bacon bits

1 Drain the potatoes and put them in the bag. Add cheese, butter, garlic powder, Italian seasoning, salt, and pepper. Close the bag and gently roll it around between your hands to coat the potatoes evenly in the butter mixture.

2 Push potatoes onto skewers and set them on a foil-covered grate over hot coals; cook until heated through and lightly browned on all sides, turning often. Slide potatoes onto a plate and sprinkle with bacon bits.

Fruity Donuts

Cut a cake donut in half to make two rings and spread a little softened cream cheese on cut sides (optional). Set sliced peaches and/or fresh blackberries on the bottom half and sprinkle with cinnamon-sugar; top with the other donut half. Wrap in greased foil and set in warm embers after your fire has burned down; cook until heated through, 4 to 7 minutes. Top with whipped cream for a scrumptious dessert.

serves 6

Flatbread Bites

Unroll a refrigerated crescent dough sheet and flatten into a thin rectangle, about 12 x 16". Cut into 18 equal pieces and arrange on a double layer of greased foil. Set foil directly on warm embers and cook slowly until bottoms are brown. Remove from heat, flip the pieces, and brush with melted butter; sprinkle with shredded Parmesan or Romano cheese, Italian seasoning, garlic salt, and red pepper flakes to taste. Return to embers and cook until golden brown. Serve with marinara sauce. *(Prefer sweet bites? After brushing dough with butter, sprinkle with cinnamon-sugar; serve with jam and white frosting.)*

serves 4

Itali-Yum Ravioli Pockets

Set a piece of Texas toast garlic bread *(thawed)* on one side of a greased pie iron, buttered side down. Open a can of mini ravioli with meatballs and spoon some of the pasta, meat, and sauce on top of the bread. Sprinkle with plenty of shredded mozzarella cheese and a little Italian seasoning; top with another piece of bread. Close the iron, trimming edges as needed, and cook on hot coals until toasted golden brown on both sides. Repeat to make three more.

Rainbow Wind Spirals

You'll Need

- Empty plastic water bottles
- Colorful permanent markers
- Scissors
- Branch or stick

More bottles, more fun!

1 Remove the labels from water bottles and be sure they are dry. Color the outside of bottles with markers *(don't use water color markers)*. Make stripes, spots, scribbles, or any patterns you want and use lots of colors.

2 Cut off the flat bottom of each bottle with scissors *(this is a good job for an adult)*.

3 Cut around the bottle from bottom to top in a slight diagonal angle to make one continuous strip, ½" to 1" wide. Stop cutting at the rounded "shoulders" of bottle. Slide the bottles onto a branch or stick, nesting them together. Then let the wind make the spirals dance!

serves 3-6

Muffin Tin Breakfast

You'll Need

12-cup muffin tin

Cooking grate

Ingredients

6 eggs

¾ C. shredded Swiss
or cheddar cheese

¾ C. chopped ham or sliced
cooked sausage links

3 C. diced potatoes *(about
2 medium)*

Diced green bell pepper

Diced onion

Salt & pepper to taste

Potato Patties

Mix 2 C. mashed potatoes, ½ C. diced red bell pepper, ¼ C. minced onion, 3 T. bacon bits, 1 T. fresh chives, 1 tsp. garlic salt, black pepper to taste, and 1 optional egg. Shape into six patties and brown on both sides in an oiled skillet set on hot embers. (Or mix 2 C. mashed sweet potatoes with 3 T. bacon bits, 1 tsp. dried thyme, 1 T. fresh parsley, 2 T. sliced green onion, ¼ tsp. red pepper flakes, and ½ tsp. garlic salt; coat in panko crumbs, then fry.)

1 Crack an egg into six greased cups of the muffin tin and stir gently with a fork to break yolks. Sprinkle some cheese and meat on each egg, using your favorite combos. Fill the other six greased cups with potatoes; add green pepper, onion, salt, and pepper as desired.

2 Cover tightly with foil and set on the grate over hot coals to cook about 15 minutes or until done, rotating once. *(Hungry? Prep and cook two muffin tins at the same time.)*

makes 8

Pizza Paws

Open a tube of refrigerated biscuits; flatten one biscuit into a paw shape, pulling off a small piece of dough. Break that piece into three little "claws" and press them onto the front of the paw. Repeat with remaining dough. Set paws on greased foil on a grate over medium coals *(or directly on warm embers)*. Cook 3 to 5 minutes, until browned on the bottom, then flip over. Top with pizza sauce, fresh mozzarella cheese, and large and small pepperoni slices to look like bear paws. Cover lightly with greased foil and cook slowly until biscuits are done and cheese melts.

serves 4

Super Tot Skewers

Thaw 30 to 40 frozen tater tots overnight in a refrigerator or cooler. Thread tots on thin skewers until full. Line them up close together on a greased griddle or foil-lined pan. Sprinkle with a little dry ranch dressing mix and your favorite shredded cheese *(we used a Mexican cheese blend, but smoked cheese would also be delish)*. Top with sliced green onions and some cooked crumbled bacon. Cover with greased foil and set on a grate over medium coals to cook until cheese is melted and everything is toasty hot, 5 to 10 minutes. Oh, so tantalizing! Oh, so addictive!

Tex-Mex Foilers

You'll Need

Foil

Cooking grate

Ingredients

2 lbs. boneless skinless chicken breasts

3 Roma tomatoes

½ C. diced onion

1 (15 oz.) can black beans, drained & rinsed

1 (15.25 oz.) can corn, drained

1 (4.25 oz.) can green chiles

2 tsp. chili powder

1 tsp. each paprika, salt, & garlic pepper

½ tsp. cumin

¼ tsp. onion powder

½ C. shredded Mexican cheese blend

Sliced green onions

Salsa

serves 4

1 Cut the chicken into 1" cubes and dice the tomatoes. Toss the chicken, tomatoes, diced onion, beans, corn, chiles, and all the seasonings into a big bowl. Stir everything together.

2 Divide the mixture among four large pieces of greased foil. Fold the foil around food and seal well. *(For smaller appetites, make smaller packs and shorten the cooking time slightly.)*

3 Place foil packs on a grate over hot coals to cook about 25 minutes or until chicken is done. Rotate packs and flip them over once or twice for even cooking. When done, open the packs and sprinkle with cheese; let melt. Sprinkle with green onions and serve with salsa.

Monkey Pies

You'll Need

Pie irons

Ingredients

Butter, softened

Bread slices

Peanut butter

Bananas, peeled & sliced

Milk chocolate *(chocolate chips, candy bar pieces, M&Ms, or chocolate-covered peanuts)*

Mini marshmallows

1 Spread butter on a slice of bread and set it in a greased pie iron, buttered side down. Smear with peanut butter and pile on banana slices, chocolate, and marshmallows.

2 Set a second slice of buttered bread on top *(buttered side up)* and close the pie iron. Trim off any excess bread crusts and cook on hot coals until golden brown on both sides. Yummy gooey goodness!

Campfire Cuppies

Spread Nutella, chocolate frosting, or peanut butter on a cupcake. Sprinkle with chocolate cookie crumb "dirt." Add a fire ring of chocolate-covered peanuts or raisins, chocolate chips, or milk chocolate rock candies. Stack some broken pretzel sticks in the middle for the firewood and add flames with yellow and orange frosting or gummy worms. (We used tubes of ready-to-use colored icing.) Sweet!

Cooking
Foil Pan

serves 4

Fireside Mac & Cheese Bowls

You'll Need

4 (4½") foil pie pans

Foil

4 long cooking sticks or branches

1 (14.5 oz.) jar light Alfredo sauce

1 C. shredded cheddar cheese

1 C. shredded mozzarella cheese

¼ to ½ C. grated Parmesan cheese

Salt & pepper to taste

Bacon bits

Ingredients

4 C. cooked & cooled macaroni

1 Coat each pie pan with cooking spray and divide the macaroni evenly among them *(about 1 cup pasta per pan).*

2 To each pan, add about ½ cup sauce, ¼ cup each cheddar and mozzarella, and 1 tablespoon Parmesan; season with salt and pepper and stir well. Sprinkle bacon bits on top and cover tightly with greased foil.

3 Wrap a big piece of foil around the whole pan like a gift, flattening and rolling two opposite sides together to make a sturdy hanging handle for each pack.

4 Slide a long stick through each handle and hold the packs over the fire. Cook 10 to 15 minutes or until cheese melts. *(If you prefer, just cook the packs on a grate over hot coals.)*

Bean Bag Toss

You'll Need

Glossy acrylic paints

Paintbrush

3 metal or aluminum pie pans

4 C. dried beans *(any kind will do)*

4 kerchiefs

Twist ties

6 to 9 long nails or screws

Toss 'em by their tails!

1 Paint the rims of the pie pans and let dry. Paint each pan a different color or assign different point values to each pan if you'd like to keep score.

2 Pour 1 cup dried beans into the center of each kerchief. Gather the corners together and twist just above the beans; secure each with a twist tie to make four balls with tails.

3 Line up the pie pans on the ground, about 2 feet apart. Pound two or three long nails through the bottom of each pan and into the ground to hold the targets in place. Step back and try to toss the bags into the pans. Score!

makes 8

Cowhorn Breakfast

You'll Need

Campfire Cooking Sticks
*(see directions next page,
or use a long fat branch
covered with foil)*

Skillet

Cooking grate

Ingredients

1 (16.3 oz.) tube Grands
biscuits *(8 ct.)*

6 eggs

6 T. water

2 T. butter

1½ C. chopped ham

1 C. shredded Swiss cheese

1 Grease the thick end of a cooking stick and wrap a biscuit around it, pinching the end closed and stretching dough to make a cowhorn shape. Cook slowly over medium coals until done, turning often; remove from stick. Repeat with remaining biscuits.

2 In a bowl, whisk the eggs with water. Set skillet on a grate over hot coals and melt the butter. Add the eggs, stirring until cooked. Mix with the ham and cheese and then fill "horns" with this combo. Serve warm.

Campfire Cooking Stick

To make a sturdy Campfire Cooking Stick, drill a 3/16" hole in one end of a 6" length of fat dowel (1 3/8" in diameter). Insert a 2-pointed screw partway into the hole and glue it in place; let dry. Drill a matching hole in the end of a long 5/8" dowel (ours was 48" long). To assemble, twist the fat dowel into the long handle. Coat the cooking end with cooking spray or vegetable oil before using.

serves 6-8

Dutch Oven Hobo Dinner

You'll Need

Deep 12" Dutch oven

Ingredients

12 ears sweet corn, husked

1½ lbs. small red potatoes

6 carrots, peeled & cut
  into chunks

1½ lbs. kielbasa or Italian
sausage, sliced *(we used
2 (13 oz.) pkgs. Italian herb
sausage)*

1 C. butter, melted

1 pt. half & half

Salt & pepper to taste

1 Stand the ears of corn on end around the inside of the Dutch oven *(trim ends as needed so they'll fit in the pot).*

2 Fill the middle of the pot with potatoes, carrots, and sausage. Drizzle melted butter and half & half over everything and season with salt and pepper.

3 Cover and set on medium coals to cook about 1 hour or until vegetables are done. Rotate the pot every 15 minutes and replenish coals as needed.

4 Pull the Dutch oven off the coals and remove the lid. Use tongs to dish up the food and then drizzle the yummy cooking liquid on top. Dig in!

What's Inside